GEMS OF IRISH HUMOUR

GEMS OF IRISH HUMOUR

by

Noel V. Ginnity

Printed by Litho Press Co., Midleton, Co. Cork.

PREFACE

"I don't know why I ask you folks to read this rubbish, you never did me any harm, although it's nice to see people laughing.

If I knew where all the smiles were kept, that made the world so gay, I'd open the door and let them out, and give them all away. And, if I knew where all the tears were kept, that make the world so grey, I'd lock the door on that store of grief and throw the key away .

I suppose I'm only a nobody, but, always remember that many a nobody, who isn't known by anybody, becomes a somebody, and is known by everybody, and everybody tells him, 'when he was a nobody, they knew he'd become a somebody someday'."

"I haven't read this book yet, but I hope it's going to be good, and if it is, I would like to thank my Father and Mother. I would also like to thank Debbie for making it possible and my two children Chaoilfhionn and Odhrán for making it necessary."

These are a collection of stories that have given me a laugh from time to time during thirty years as a funny man. They have been collected by me. Some written for me and some written by me. Some heard by me in many parts of Ireland and throughout the world. some may even have been told by you!

In this book I hope you will find some stories that will make you smile. I have told these stories with great success in many parts of the world, on T.V., Radio and Stage.

Why not pick out one's you like, try them on your friends, if you touch their funny bone, you will be keeping in motion one of the greatest mysteries of Life, The Gift of Laughter.

Noel V. Ginnity.

But why worry.   Life is a funny proposition. Many a person comes into this world, without his consent, and leaves it against his will.

On earth he is misjudged and misunderstood. In infancy he's an angel. In manhood he's a devil.

If he has a wife and family he is a mug. If he's a bachelor he is considered inhuman.

If he walks into a public house, he's a drunkard. If he stays out of it, he's a miserable so and so.

If he is poor, he has no brains. If he is rich, he is considered smart but dishonest, and has all the luck in the world.

If he gives to charity, he does it for advertisement. If he doesn't he is mean and stingy.

When he comes into this world everyone wants to kiss him, and before he leaves everyone wants to kick him.

If he dies young, he had a great future before him, if he lives to a ripe old age everybody hopes he has made his will.

So always remember, where there is a will there are always relations.

* * * * * * * * * *

Did you hear about the Irish test tube baby – he was born in a bottle of Guinness – he had a very slender body, but he had a lovely head on him.

* * * * * * * * * *

A girl went to the dentist, she said "My God! I would rather have a baby than have my teeth out". The dentist said, "Make up your mind before I tilt the chair".

* * * * * * * * * *

My friend is just back from Moscow – I don't like them Russians, they have nothing, and, want to share it with everyone.

Anyway, my friend wanted to buy a car, so he went to the showrooms. There were no cars there, the salesman showed him one in a catalogue and said "We can have this for you in ten years – we are very prompt here". "Ten years" my friend said "Well!, will it be in the morning or the afternoon?" The salesman said, "Why is it important to know if it is in the morning or the afternoon". My friend said "Because I'm expecting the plumber in the morning".

* * * * * * * * * *

Mr and Mrs Casey were married for twelve years and had no children. One day the Parish priest called around and told them he was going to Rome. Mrs Casey asked him to light a candle for her that she might have some children. Years later, the priest arrives back in Ireland and calls on Mrs Casey, only to find the house full of children, and no Mr. Casey. He asks "Where is Mr. Casey?" she says, "He is gone to Rome to blow out that bloody candle".

* * * * * * * * * *

Murphy was not feeling too well, so he decided to go to the doctor. The doctor examined him and said, "I have got some bad new for you, your going to have to take a pill for the rest of your life". Murphy said, "That is not too bad at all". The doctor said, "I am only giving you six."

* * * * * * * * * *

My wife is a strange lady. I came home from work the other evening and I caught her in bed with three men. I said, "Hello, hello, Hello," she said, "What's wrong, are you not talking to me?"

* * * * * * * * * *

My wife is so fat, no matter where she sits down she's beside you.

* * * * * * * * * *

Murphy: "I just got this telegram from my wife. I don't know what to do. It says she has just given birth to triplets and we don't have any money."

Casey: "Well, why don't you go to work and make some money. Can you drive a truck?"

Murphy: "No"

Casey: "Can you wait on tables?"

Murphy: "No"

Casey: "Can you dig ditches?"

Murphy: "No"

Casey: "What can you do?"

Murphy: "Did you not read the telegram?"

* * * * * * * * * *

Murphy: "Why did you die? Why did you die? Why did you die?"

Casey: "Why did who die. Your wife?"

Murphy: "No"

Casey: "Your sister?"

Murphy: "No"

Casey: "Well, who then?"

Murphy: "My wife's first husband.
            Why did you die? Why did
            you die?"

* * * * * * * * * *

Murphy came out and looked around the
floor of the stage for something.
Casey: "What are you looking for?

Murphy: "A diamond ring"

Casey: "Where did you loose it?"

Murphy: "Backstage"

Casey: "Then why are you looking
            for it out here?"

Murphy: "More Light"

* * * * * * * * * *

A pal of mine, a small farmer, had a visit
from the Income Tax man the other day,
and, taking out a form, said "And how
many workers and dependants have
you". Murphy said, "There is the wife
and the five kids, the wife's mother and
father, and me own mother and father,
and the old eejit who get five shillings a
week". the tax man said, "What does the
old eejit do?" Murphy said, "he gets up a

five in the morning, brings in the cows, milks them and takes them back to the meadow, he then takes the milk to the creamery, when he comes back , he cleans up the barn, feeds the hens and collects the eggs. Then he snags the turnips, feeds the pigs, cuts some turf at the bog, cuts a bit of corn, and, in his spare time he ploughs a couple of ten acre fields, and by that time it is usually so dark that he gets lost on the way home". The Tax man said, "I'd like to meet this old eejit", Murphy said, "You'd like to meet him, you're talking to him".

* * * * * * * * * *

Farmer said to Pat. "Put the sheep in the pens, so that I can count them" After he did so, the farmer said "That's a hare", Pat said, "I'll know the next time, it took me two hours to catch that fellow".

The first day he was using the milking machine, he got a short circuit and got four buckets of steam.
He was an important fellow with the cows, he was the chief squirt.

He once crossed a hen with centipede, and, got a chicken with eight legs. The only trouble he had was catching him.

I went to see a pal of mine the other day. I said, "How are you feeling", He said, "Not too good," I said, "That is bad," He said, "Well, it's not too bad, I just got married," I said, "that's good," He said, "Well it's not too good, the wife is very mean," I said, "Well that's bad," He said, "Well it's not too bad, she bought me an old house", I said, "Well, that's good" he said, "Well it's not too good, the house was burned down last night", I said, "Well, that's bad", He said, "Well it's not too bad, she was in it".

* * * * * * * * * *

Smith has not been the same since he walked into a shooting gallery with a clay pipe in his mouth.

The other day he fell from the top of a seven storey building and landed at Murphy's feet. Murphy, "What happened?" Smith said, "I don't know, just got here myself".

* * * * * * * * * *

The minute my mother-in-law knocks on the door, I know it's her, because the canary stops singing, and, the mice throw themselves on the traps.

She is so ugly, she has a face on her like a bulldog chewing a wasp.

I don't mind telling you, I am afraid of her. If ever I come home from the pub with a few drinks on me and I know she is there, I always take my clothes off downstairs, and walk up the stairs backways, so if she meets me, I can say I am going down stairs for a drink of water.

* * * * * * * * * *

What about the Kerryman who locked his keys in the car.
It took him 2 hours with a coat hanger to get his family out.

* * * * * * * * * *

While I was in America, I was amazed at all the money given away on the television quiz programmes. Millions of dollars. In Ireland, we have only one little quiz programme. The top prize is a steam iron, or £15.

Here are some of the questions - with the replies that Murphy gave.

Quiz Master: Could you tell me Gandhi's first name?

Murphy: Would it be Goosey Goosey!

Quiz Master: Where was Anne Bolen beheaded?

Murphy: Was it below the neck?

Quiz Master: Where do you get Virgin wool?

Murphy: From ugly sheep.

Quiz Master: Where is Uganda?

Murphy: Down in Killarney, with me Granma

Quiz Master: Could you name two days of the week beginning with the letter "T"?

Murphy: Today and Tomorrow.

Quiz Master: Could you please spell Paint?

Murphy: Which colour?

Quiz Master: Name four fruits beginning with the letter "T"?

Murphy: Tomato, Tangerine, Tin of Pears and a Tin of Peaches.

Quiz Master: What nationality was God?

Murphy: An Irishman, because at the age of 33, he was single, unemployed and living with his mother.

Quiz Master: Could you give me a sentence with a noun in it?

Murphy: I like a drink now and then.

Quiz Master: What is a Jumbo jet?

Murphy: Would it be an elephant, with his leg up against the wall.

* * * * * * * * * *

Smith and Kelly got on a train in Dublin. The collector looked at the tickets and said, "This train is going to Kerry, you're on the wrong train" Out like a flash, had a couple more drinks for the road, (rather strange for Irishmen) and back into another train. The collector said, "This train is going to Galway, you're on the wrong train". Out again, and naturally another few drinks for the road. Back they went to another carriage and sitting opposite them was an old clergyman. he looked at the two men and said, "you two are on the road to hell". Smith said, "Well, would you believe it, we're on the wrong train again".

I know one critic who is so narrow minded, he can look through a keyhole with both eyes.

* * * * * * * * * *

I can't even insure my jokes. They've died too often.

* * * * * * * * * *

I once was in a crowded elevator when a woman let out a terrific scream. Then a little boy looked up at his mother and said, "I don't care, it was in my face, so I bit it."

* * * * * * * * * *

A lot of trouble in my marriage was caused by her mother. My wife said to me last week, "Can my mother come down for the week-end? I said, "Why?" She said, "She is sick of the attic".

* * * * * * * * * *

An abbot asked a novice monk to produce an illuminated manuscript. That night he broke into Trinity College and set fire to the Book of Kells.

* * * * * * * * * *

Mulligan was in confession, "It's really about my wife, Father. She takes me to the pub every night and knocks back about twenty pints of porter. How do I deal with a fallen woman?"
Priest: "Have you tried stepping over her".

* * * * * * * * * *

Murphy had taken up boxing and was hammered unconscious in the first bout. he left the ring in a desperate state. Next morning he staggered into the doctor's surgery and groaned, "My eyesight, Doc. I can't even see me hands in front of me face" The doctor looked up impatiently

19

and said, "go home and take your boxing gloves off".

* * * * * * * * * *

Our parish priest is so absent minded. The other day he put his own dog collar on his Alsatian by mistake.
You could tell, because the damn thing was barking in Latin.

* * * * * * * * * *

Murphy was coming home last St. Patrick's day, and, had had a right few drinks. The police stopped him and said, "We have reason to believe, you have been drinking".
Murphy said, "I don't remember seeing you in any of the pubs. Anyway, that's right, I started off with half a bottle of whiskey and went on and had 10 pints". The police man said, "Would you mind blowing into this bag". Murphy said, "Why, Do you not believe me?".

* * * * * * * * * *

We have to work at our marriage, we go out two nights a week for a candle-light dinner. She goes Tuesday and I go Thursday.

* * * * * * * * * *

What about the guy who had a plastic hip operation.
He asked the doctor for the bone for his dog.

* * * * * * * * * *

Mulligan goes into the psychiatrist's office in a distressed state: "Doctor, I keep dressing up as a nun".
Psychiatrist: "It's a habit you'll have to get out of".

* * * * * * * * * *

We had a blessed event in our house to-day. My mother-in-law broker her leg and we had to shoot her.

* * * * * * * * * *

We were very poor. There were 8 of us in the one bed. I did not know what it was like to sleep on my own until I got married.

* * * * * * * * * *

Remember what it was like the day you got married. The photographer wanted to take photos of the happy couple.
Her and her mother.

* * * * * * * * * *

I came down for breakfast the other morning. The wife said, "What do you want for breakfast?" I said, "I will have a boiled egg". She said, "O.K. but there is no water, so you can't have any tea or coffee." To this day, I still don't know how she boiled that egg. It is the luck of God, I didn't ask her for a poached egg.

* * * * * * * * * *

Casey bought a new pair of shoes. They were so tight, he had to wear them for a week before he could get his feet into them.

* * * * * * * * * *

My father's car was so bad, every Sunday he used to take us out for a push.

* * * * * * * * * *

We were such a large family, when we went out on a Sunday, people used to think Mass was over.

* * * * * * * * * *

My wife's mouth was so big. she could whisper in her own ear.

* * * * * * * * * *

My wife said, "I have the face of a fourteen year old" I said, "Well if I were you I would give it back to her, you are wrinkling it up on her."

* * * * * * * * * *

When the Lord created man he only gave him 20 years of normal sex life. He then created the monkey and gave him 20 years of sex life. The monkey said "Ten's enough for me" and, man stepped in and said, I'll take the other ten". He then created the lion and gave him 20 years. The lion also said "Ten is enough" and Man once again said "I will have the other ten". And, lastly the Jack-Ass. He

23

got 20 years and he said to the Lord, "Ten's enough for me" Man again stepped in and said "I'll have the other ten."

And, that is the way I see it.

Man with 20 years of normal sex life. Ten years of monkeying about with it. Ten years lying (lion) about it. And, the last ten making a Jack-ass of himself.

* * * * * * * * * *

When Murphy's father died, all he left him was an old Ass. Murphy decided to raffle it, at a £1 a ticket. By the time he had sold all the tickets, the ass died. His wife said, "Everybody will be mad at you", "Not at all" said Murphy, "only the winner, so I'll give him his money back".

* * * * * * * * * *

Did you hear the story about the couple who got married and slept back to back. She was a Catholic and he was a Protestant, and neither would turn.

* * * * * * * * * *

When a friend of mine got home, the other night, blind drunk. His wife hit the ceiling. Six feet lower and the bullet would have gone clean through him.

* * * * * * * * * *

A man I know advertised for a wife, and was absolutely astounded when back came three thousand replies.
Most of which said, "You can have mine".

* * * * * * * * * *

Talk about luck. My wife just ran off with a chap I owe money to.

* * * * * * * * * *

Casey opened a small grocer shop, and, Abel Cohen opened in opposition across the road. Casey was selling butter for 60p a lb. So, Abel put a notice in the window, "butter 50 a lb." Casey changed his sign to 40 p a lb, and then Cohen changed his price to 30p a lb. Casey went bust, and closed his shop. He went to Cohen and said, "congratulations Mr. Cohen, I don't know how you can sell butter at 30p a lb". Cohen said, "I don't sell butter".

* * * * * * * * * *

If it hadn't been for the children, the wife and I would have separated long ago. She wouldn't take them and neither would I.

* * * * * * * * * *

A pal of mine has a small grocery shop in Mullingar. Recently, two huge Super-markets opened, one on either side of him. he solved his problem by putting a new sign over his shop. It says MAIN ENTRANCE.

* * * * * * * * * *

I must get a new cheque book. There's no money left in the old one. My main trouble is that when I get my wages, there is always too much week left over at the end of the money.

* * * * * * * * * *

There's nothing like a nice seaside holiday for enjoying yourself. The weather was gorgeous . . . I took off my shirt, and then my vest. The wife was glaring at me. "Put your shirt back on again" she insisted, looking around at all the other couples. "People will think I married you for your money."

* * * * * * * * * *

I was such an ugly baby, the doctor slapped everyone.

I was caesarian born. It has no ill effects on me except every time I leave the house, I go out by the window.

I was such an ugly baby, I have pictures of my parents leaving the hospital, with sacks over their heads.

My father came to the hospital, "is it a boy or a girl?" The doctor said "No". Then the nurse said, "it is a little boy!" My father was delighted. The nurse said, "I would not get too excited, if I was you, that is the smallest child born here, for the past 27 years". My father said, "Ah, sure I was not expecting much, sure I am only three weeks married".

I came from a large family, there were 21 children. They could never figure out whether my mother was a good Catholic or a sloppy Protestant.

I was the youngest, I had 20 sisters, can you imagine the hand-me-down situation. At the age of 12, I was going to school in a little black and white dress. The teacher was furious, he was wearing one the same.

As my sisters got older, things actually got worse for me. I had to wear all their slacks and pants and jeans. One day I was wearing a pair of jeans belonging to my sister, it had a big pocket in the front and a zipper along the side. I was nearly arrested just looking for change.

* * * * * * * * * *

Murphy was not feeling too well, so he decided to go to the doctor. She asked him, did he smoke. He said, "I do, 150 a day." She said, "You won't live 3 months". He said, "I want another opinion." She said, "You are ugly as well."

* * * * * * * * * *

Murphy then decided to go to a male doctor instead. When he arrived, the doctor told him to take off all his clothes and go into a room. There was another man in the room with nothing on him either. I said, "This is a funny doctor, I have just a cold, and he told me to take off all my clothes". The other man said, "you think that is bad, I am only here to tune the piano".
Murphy went to the doctor and he said, "I have some bad news for you, and some very very bad news for you" Murphy

said, "Give me the bad new first". "O.K. you have 24 hours to live, and the very bad news is, I should have told you yesterday".

* * * * * * * * * *

I was born in Ireland at the head of the stairs. I was a step child. I was born on my mother's wedding anniversary. She was disappointed. She was expecting a fur coat.

* * * * * * * * * *

Mulligan: I suppose you think I'm a perfect idiot?"

Murphy: "No one is perfect"

* * * * * * * * * *

Mother: "If you wanted to go fishing, why didn't you come and ask me first."

Boy: "Because, I wanted to go fishing".

* * * * * * * * * *

Teacher: "Where are the Andes?"

Boy: "At the end of your wristies!"

* * * * * * * * * *

A peeping Tom came up before the judge. The Judge said, "What is your name?" He said, "Curtains" The Judge said, "Go home and pull yourself together".

* * * * * * * * * *

A young lady was having a bath when there was a knock at the door. She said, "Who is it?" The answer came back, "A blind sales man." She jumped up and opened the door and the man said, " I've come to fit the Venetian blinds".

* * * * * * * * * *

Paddy went out to the bar and sat down to have a drink when a fight broke out and this fellow had his nose broken off. I saved his life, I stuck it back on and ran all the way with him to the hospital. It was pouring rain. When we arrived, he was dead. He had drowned. I had stuck his nose on upside down.

* * * * * * * * * *

The other evening when I was driving her home, I asked her what would she really like for her birthday. She said, "A little plot in the church yard" I could not refuse her request. I adored the ground that was coming to her. The other day, she said, "What are you going to buy me for Xmas," I said, "You have not used your birthday present yet."

* * * * * * * * * *

I walked into a Chinese restaurant the other day with my kilt on. The manager bowed very low in front of me. I said, "You Cantonese". He said, "No, me Peeping".

* * * * * * * * * *

Heard about the China man who went to Ireland and changed his name to Paddy Fields.

* * * * * * * * * *

Of course I am Scots. On me mother's side.
I am Irish by a friend of me fathers.

* * * * * * * * * *

I met the wife years ago in a dance hall. She was the most beautiful girl on the dance floor. Then she got up and rolled her eyes at me, I rolled them back to her.

Then she sent the waiter over to ask me for a dance, he danced very well for a waiter.

She sat on the balcony, smoking a clay pipe, she looked as if she was out of this world, which is quite understandable, considering there was no balcony in the dance hall. She was too drunk to notice. She was surrounded by male admirers, some wanting to talk, others wanting to light her pipe. She kissed me so passionately, smoke came out of her ears. She knocked out two of my front teeth, she forgot to take the pipe out of her mouth.

* * * * * * * * * *

My wife was knock-kneed, and played the cello. Side saddle of course. You might call her a virtuoso, but she was quite respectable. If they could have straightened her legs she'd have been six feet tall.

* * * * * * * * * *

We had her mother for dinner last Sunday, she tasted terrible. She was celebrating the 15th anniversary of her 60th birthday. She said, "How old do you think I look" I could not believe it her face looked as if it had worn out five bodies. I bought her a hat for her birthday, she said "this hat is not fit for a pig". I said "O.K. I'll take this back and get you one that is". I was going to get her something else, but it needed a prescription. I don't know what to call her, but in India, she'd be sacred. She said, "When you die, I'm going to dance on your grave" I said. "I hope you do, I'm being buried at sea."

* * * * * * * * * *

Who's job is it???

This is a story about four people named Everybody, Somebody, Anybody and Nobody.

There was an important job to be done, and Everybody was sure Somebody would do it. Anybody could have done it, but Nobody did it. Somebody got angry about that, because it was Everybody's job. Everybody thought Anybody could do it, but Nobody realised that Everybody wouldn't do it.

It ended that Everybody blamed Somebody, when Nobody did what Anybody could have done.

* * * * * * * * * *

Murphy's wife was always getting on to him for coming home late, the other night he arrived home late. There was a letter on the mantlepiece, waiting for him. It read, "Dear Pat, the night before last you came home yesterday, last night you came home this morning, if you come home tomorrow, today, you're not sleeping in this house tonight."

* * * * * * * * * *

Murphy suffered from insomnia, he could not sleep either. He said to his doctor, "What is a good thing for insomnia" the doctor said, "A good nights sleep." Murphy said, "I will have to try that". Fair enough" said the doctor,. "and if that does not work, take this box of pills, and if you can not sleep, get the wife to wake you every half hour and give you one."

* * * * * * * * * *

Murphy had a farm. He owned two cows and a bull. I said, "Those two cows look identical" "Yes", he said, "And they look alike too – Especially the one on the left."

* * * * * * * * * *

He was milking a cow the other day, when all of a sudden the bull came charging into the field. I shouted a warning, but Murphy took no notice. The bull got to within two feet of Murphy, when he stopped dead in his tracks, and went back across the field. I said, "Were you not afraid" He said, "No it was the bull that was afraid, you see I was milking his mother-in-law."

* * * * * * * * * *

Murphy was up in Dublin, when he saw an ostrich egg in a shop window. He walked in and said, "That's an Ostrich egg, what make is it?" The shop keeper said, "It's an Australian greyhounds egg." Murphy bought it for ten shillings, took it home to the village, put it on the bar counter and said, "It's an Australian greyhound's egg, how am I going to hatch it." Casey said, "Take it up to the top of the Mountains of Mourne, and let it roll down and the friction will hatch it out". Well, they started the egg rolling from the top of mountain, and halfway down there was a big Blarney stone sticking up, and there was a little hare sheltering behind it. The egg hit the stone and the contents went all over the hare. It took off at full speed. Murphy said, "Look at the speed of it, and him only a pup!"

* * * * * * * * * *

Murphy was not feeling too well, the doctor told him, he'd have to sleep in the open, so he got a job in the police force. The first day he was on duty, he saw a car coming towards him, he put up his hand and said, "Halt, and, Stop as well" he said to the fella, "Have you a driving licence." The fella said, "I have: Murphy said, "It's a good job you have, because if you hadn't I'd want to see it".

* * * * * * * * * *

A few years ago, I met this marvellous doctor. He got his Degree from the same correspondence school that Ian Paisley did. It's a place in America, The Sylvester Stallone College of Fine Art & Ballet Academy! it operates out of an air vent in Brooklyn!

Of course, Paisley did a different course. He did advanced Bigotry and farmyard impressions.

When I met him he had just become a surgeon. We did not meet in a hospital. He was working part time in a butcher's shop in Sligo, So I went to see him. He said, "What's the problem?" I said, "I'm diminutive." Well, he started to get his Latin books down to look it up, so I thought – We've got a one-syllable man here – better keep it simple. I said, "Put it this way – if people were eggs, I'd be grade 15!" I could see he was working hard on this one – even his ears were frowning!

* * * * * * * * * *

Speaking of kids, I was coming into the factory and saw a little girl, about eight years of age, smoking a cigarette. I said, "Does your mother know you smoke?" she said "Yes, and does your mother know you speak to strange little girls!"

* * * * * * * * * *

Mrs Mulligan was filling in a hire purchase agreement, when the assistant asked her to sign her name.
Mrs Mulligan fumbled and mumbled for a minute or so.
she then admitted that she could not.

Assistant: "Well, make an 'X' instead"
Mrs. Mulligan nodded, and made her mark.

Assistant: "But you have put the letter 'Z'
Mrs. Mulligan: "Sorry, Ma'm, my mistake . . . I've gone and put me maiden name."

* * * * * * * * * *

A Catholic boy was peering into a Baptist Chapel, when he noticed a statue of the Good Shepherd.
He whispered to the lad beside him, "Surely a Protestant church can't have the same good Shepherd as ours?"
His friend replied, pointing at the baptismal pool, "And, why not? They've got a sheep – dip for the flock, haven't they"

* * * * * * * * * *

A football team of young priests were about to kick-off, against a side of Methodist ministers. Just before the game commenced, all the priests knelt down and prayed to Our Lady for guidance and skill. At the final whistle, the score was 43 - 0 in favour of the Methodists. Said one of the ministers, "That proves what little Our Lady can do for anyone" A priest replied, "Nonsense. It just proves what little a woman knows about football".

* * * * * * * * * *

Reilly, working in England, decided to go home. Sent a telegram to his wife saying "Meet me at the station". When he arrived, she was not there. he rushed home to find his wife sitting on the lodger's knee. He walked out and started to drink in the nearest pub. Next thing he felt a tap on his shoulder. It was the wife's father. He said, "Pat, you're making a big mistake, there is a logical explanation, if you'll only listen" Pat said, "O.K. what is the explanation?" The father said, "She did not get your telegram."

* * * * * * * * * *

I asked Pat why he looked so miserable? He said, "Every time I go home, my wife's three brothers beat me up" I said, "Why do you not flare up and be a man?" He said, "How: I said, "Come along with me and have a drink, then go home and be King of your own castle" Murphy got plastered, and home he went. The next day I said, "How did you get on?" He said, "I went home and believe it or not, I gave her three brothers such a hiding, that two of them could not go to school this morning."

* * * * * * * * * *

Hear about the heavy weight boxer on his honeymoon. Every time his wife touched him on the shoulder, he broke and went to a neutral corner.

* * * * * * * * * *

She used to be a bonnie lassie, but now she is just a bonny chassis.

She has so many wrinkles in her forehead, she has to screw her hat on.

* * * * * * * * * *

This is the story of a rather henpecked husband, who went to town every morning on business. This particular morning his wife insisted on going with him. That evening she said she would like to go to the Cork a Too Club. he said, "We can't go there, think of my reputation" But she insisted. He knocked at the door of the club, a little peep hole opened and a girl said, "Come in Charlie", Inside, the cloakroom girl said, "Hiya Charlie". The waiter said "the usual corner". Just as they sat down a beautiful redhead came over and threw her arms around his neck and said, "Charlie darling". His wife said, "let's get out of here", she hailed a taxi and got in. The wife raising her voice said, "It was bad enough all those other characters, saying hello Charlie, but that redhead, I'm disgusted" With that the driver pulled the slide back and said, "Picked the wrong one, tonight, Charlie."

* * * * * * * * * *

Pat said to Mike, "How's your father" Mike said, "he's fading away" he said, "You know how thin I am, and you know how thin you are, well, he is twice as thin as the two of our bodies put together".

* * * * * * * * * *

I met him at the races the other day all dolled up, with a pair of binoculars in his hands, sitting beside me in the stands. He's only a little fellow. I said, "What's in front?" He said, "A fellow with a bowler hat".

* * * * * * * * * *

In the second race, the bookies were shouting, "Five to Four the favourite". Casey was shouting, "Twenty to one a dead heat" I said, "Twenty to one a dead heat, Where the hell were you looking?" He said, "Over there". It was two horses pulling a plough.

* * * * * * * * * *

My wife is so innocent. She thought iced lolly, was Eskimo money. She thought, Forever Amber was a hold up on a pedestrian crossing.

My pet name for her is Flour. She's been through the mill.

* * * * * * * * * *

She had three sisters on her mother's side. And, three mothers on her father's side.

Before she was married they used to call her muscles. She was in everybodys arms.

My grandmother went on the Pill last Tuesday, she is 84 she does not want any more grand children.

* * * * * * * * * *

She went into a drug store and said "I want the Pill, and could you mash it up for me". "Oh, he said, "You don't mash it up, you swallow it with water." She said, "Mash it up, Mash it up". So he mashed it up, and, she sprinkled it on the back of her hand and proceeded to sniff it up her nose, saying "Sure, at my age, its all in my head".

* * * * * * * * * *

My father is 89, some one told my mother he was out chasing women, she said "Why should I worry, dogs chase cars, but they can't drive".

* * * * * * * * * *

Things are so bad here in Ireland, when they are playing Bingo, they call the numbers out in Latin, so the Protestants can't win.

* * * * * * * * * *

It is 41 years since the last war, Thank God! You know my father, he never really recovered from the effects of the last war. He fought in Germany, Poland and France, he could not agree with anybody.

* * * * * * * * * *

My friend Murphy was being lowered in to a well the other evening. He got nervous and shouted up, "Stop lowering me or I will cut the rope".

* * * * * * * * * *

He was held up the other night, and the bandit said, "Your money or your life," Murphy said, "Take my life, I'm saving my money for my old age".

* * * * * * * * * *

He went out shooting with Smith the other day. Smith said, "I will have a shot at this Rook" Murphy said, "How do you know that's a Rook", Smith said, "that's easy, if you see a lot of Rooks together them's Crows, but if you see a Crow by itself then that's a Rook".

* * * * * * * * * *

My friend Reilly does a wonderful job. He used to take empty horse boxes to the races, he used to take the non-runners.

* * * * * * * * * *

Paddy was watching a Communist meeting in Hyde Park. The speaker spotting him, called him over, and said to the crowd, "Now here is a fine man" and, addressing him self to Paddy, said, "If you were a Communist and had £2,000, would you give one to your comrades?" "I would" said Paddy. "If you had two cows, would you give one to your comrades?" "I would indeed" said Paddy. "If you had two greyhounds, would you give one to your comrades?". "Well", said Paddy, "I would have to think about that one," "Why" said the Communist. "Because" said Paddy, "I've got two greyhounds."

* * * * * * * * * *

Pat went to the doctor and said "I would like to live to be 100." The doctor said, "Do you smoke?" Pat said "No", "Drink?" "No". "Are you fond of the ladies?" "I could not care less" answered Pat. "Well" said the doctor, "Why the hell, do you want to live to be 100?"

* * * * * * * * * *

Murphy did a bit of boxing in his day. He fought under the name Rembrant. Rembrant, he was on the canvas so often.

* * * * * * * * * *

I'd rather have ten kids than a million dollars.
A guy with a million dollars wants another million, and another million after that.
But a guy with ten kids . . .

* * * * * * * * * *

You know, it took Juliet seven years to get Romeo to propose. It just proves the old saying: Romeo wasn't made in a day!

* * * * * * * * * *

Remember when you first started to shave. With a tweezers and a magnifying glass.

* * * * * * * * * *

I always use a dial phone,
With me it never fails;
I never get my number,
But it manicures my nails.

* * * * * * * * * *

So, remember that old Chinese saying: If dog lead man, he blind. If man lead dog, he married.

* * * * * * * * * *

Adam was the luckiest man in history. No mother in law.

* * * * * * * * * *

They say 80% of the work is being done by machines.
So how come everyone is so tired at night.

* * * * * * * * * *

There is only one difference between an umbrella and a woman. You can shut up an umbrella.

* * * * * * * * * *

At least there's one good thing about Hell. No one down there can tell you where to go.

* * * * * * * * * *

Never run after a bus or a woman. There'll be another along in a minute. Maybe there aren't so many after midnight, but the ones you get are faster.

* * * * * * * * * *

You've got to give cannibals credit. They're always trying to get a head.

* * * * * * * * * *

It was Robinson Crusoe who started the forty hour week.
He had all his work done by Friday.

* * * * * * * * * *

Some people like to eat crackers in bed.
I prefer a roll with honey.

* * * * * * * * * *

Sometimes it helps to be bald. If you are
on a sofa with a girl, and her mother
walks in, all you have to do is to
straighten your tie.

* * * * * * * * * *

My mother was so poor, we could not
even afford laxatives.
She used to put us on a line of potties (the
whole 21 of us) and she would tell us
ghost stories.

* * * * * * * * * *

Two tourists were visiting our National
Art gallery in Dublin one Russian and
one Frenchman. They were discussing
the painting of Adam and Eve by
Caravagio. The Russian said, "Adam and
Eve were Russian, they have only one
apple and they are sharing it". The
Frenchman said, "No, No, they were
French, they have no clothes on, they are
going to make love," an Irishman
overheard their conversation and said
"Not at all, Adam and Eve were Irish,
That is Adam and Eve Murphy. Look,

they have no clothes, no food, and, they think they are in Heaven."

* * * * * * * * * *

Unemployment is very bad all over the world. It is very bad in Ireland. I was lying in bed last week looking for work and I said to the wife's sister, "It is very foggy out there" she said, "Are you not going out to look for work, it is clearing over the roof tops," I said, "Sure I won't be going that way."

* * * * * * * * * *

If there were only three women left in the world, two would have their heads together talking about the other one.

* * * * * * * * * *

There are two kinds of lawyers . . . Those who know the law, and those who know the Judge.

* * * * * * * * * *

At 20, women are like Africa . . . Hot and tempestuous!
At 45, women are like Europe . . . Crumbling, but still interesting!
At 70, women are like Australia . . . Everybody knows where it is, but who wants to go there?

* * * * * * * * * *

They say laugh and the whole world laughs with you.
I'd rather cry and sell 3,000,000 books.

* * * * * * * * * *

I lived in a very rough area. If you saw a cat with his tail on, you knew he was a tourist.

* * * * * * * * * *

There's a lot of violence in the world today. My brother is into karate. He has a black belt. He said to me, "I will teach you karate" I said, "No, I hate any form of violence, boxing, karate, kung fu, anything like that I just hate it" He said, "I will teach you the sounds instead of the actions" A few weeks later, I was in a bar in Dublin, when, this big man, he was about 6' 6" and covered with hair from head to toe. Now you would think his mother was after knitting him. He knocked over my drink. I thought, this is my chance to use my sounds in karate. I drew myself up to my full height and I looked him straight in the knee and said "Ah!, Fu, King Fu, Karate" . . . He killed me stone dead. He was Deaf.

* * * * * * * * * *

The slowest person on earth is a nudist going through a barbed-wire fence.

* * * * * * * * * *

Don't get married to avoid the draft. It's better to spend a couple of years with a rifle, than the rest of your life, with a battle-axe.

* * * * * * * * * *

What I want to know is, why didn't Noah step on those two bed bugs when they stepped into the Ark?

* * * * * * * * * *

He got a job as a mechanic, but he kept doing his nut.
He worked as a carpenter and he kept biting his nails.

* * * * * * * * * *

I went over to work in England last year. I did very badly over there. I nearly starved to death. I was reduced to begging and knocking on peoples' doors looking for money and food. I knocked on this woman's door, and I said, "Mrs, I have not eaten a thing for four weeks," she said, "Well, you would want to try and force yourself." She said, "Would you like some of yesterday's soup?" "I would" I said, "Well, then come back tomorrow" she said.

* * * * * * * * * *

My friend went to the doctor last week. The doctor said, "There's nothing wrong with you, it is just a little bit of tension, from your days work. This is what you should do when you get home from work. Just fetch the wife and go upstairs for a little bit of relaxation." He thanked the doctor and off he went. Three weeks later, he met the doctor. "That was a fantastic cure, Doctor, and I must say, you have a lovely house as well."

* * * * * * * * * *

My friend Reilly, is a steady worker. In fact if he was any steadier he would be motionless.

The other day the foreman said "Reilly, fetch me a wheelbarrow". Reilly came back pulling a barrow with another one on top. The foreman said, "I only asked for one". Reilly said, "I know, but you did not expect me to carry it."

* * * * * * * * * *

He got a job in a candle factory but he packed it in.
It got on his wick.

* * * * * * * * * *

He said to a farmer "Can you use me on the land."
The farmer said, "No, we've got stuff for that."

* * * * * * * * * *

He got a job on the railways.
The station master said, "Why are the gates only half open"
"Because" said Reilly, "We are only half expecting a train."

* * * * * * * * * *

Isn't it wonderful? No matter where a filling station decides to put its pumps, they always find gas!

* * * * * * * * * *

Girls can be awful nice when they want!

* * * * * * * * * *

To-day, everything is speed. Even money goes faster than it used to.

* * * * * * * * * *

It's a great life, if you don't week-end.

* * * * * * * * * *

What's the use of working? If your ship does come in, you'll find all y o u r relatives standing on the docks.

* * * * * * * * * *

They say there are 50% more men in mental hospitals than women. That may be so, but who put them there?

* * * * * * * * * *

There's one good thing about going to hell.
It's downhill all the way.

* * * * * * * * * *

I had my first date when I was 14. She was nearly six feet tall, and she had beautiful legs. When I walked her home after the pictures, I wanted to show her how romantic I was, so I stood on my toes and gave her a long, lingering kiss . . . on the knees.

I'll never forget the day I married the wife. (No matter how hard I try). There we were, standing side by side on the altar, when the priest said, that he couldn't start the ceremony until the bridegroom got up off his knees.

* * * * * * * * * *

Two nuns went to a football game there were two Punk Rockers behind them and they started to give them a hard time. One punk Rocker said "I wish could go to England there is only 15% Catholics there." The other Punk Rocker said, "I wish I could go to Belfast there is only 5% Catholics there." One of the nuns turned around and said, "I wish you could go to hell there are no Catholics there.

* * * * * * * * * *

Rev. Mother on her death bed and she is surrounded by all the nuns who are trying to force milk passed her lips, a arrives saying that milk is no good give her a drop of Irish whiskey, so they topped up the milk with whiskey and gave it to the Rev. Mother who seemed to enjoy it, a sparkle came into her eye for a few moments then she seemed to fade away again, the nuns draw closer to her and say, "Have you any advice to give us before you depart for heaven", The Rev. Mother says, "For God's sake don't sell that cow."

* * * * * * * * * *

"The trouble with being small,
Is very plain to see.
For people who are very tall
Keep looking down at me.
But when I see a woman in a mini-skirt it's true.
I nearly get a heart-attack . . .
Oh! brother, what a view."

* * * * * * * * * *

I was so small when I was born that me Mother didn't even have labour pains . . . she just hiccoughed, and there I was.

Then the nurse lifted me up by the ankles and accidently dropped me . . . They spent two hours searching the operating theatre before they discovered that I was after falling up her sleeve.

When they brought me home I was too small to sleep in a cot, so me ould fella fixed up a bed for me in a shoe-box in front of the fire. It was alright, until, the cat came in . . . picked me up by the back of me neck, in her mouth, and took me out to the shed with the other kittens.

When I started to use the toilet they had to put a rope ladder on the inside, so that I could climb out when I was finished.

I was the only kid in the school who carried his lunch in a matchbox.

* * * * * * * * * *

An Irishman was leaning against an oil tank on a huge Oil Rig when the Captain rushed over and said. "For God sake, man, don't you know you shouldn't be smoking." Casey said, "Please don't worry about me, I don't inhale."

Suddenly, he began to jump up and down. The Captain said, "Now what are you doing" Casey said, "I took medicine this morning, and I forgot to shake the bottle."

* * * * * * * * * *

Hear about the Irish dog that walked backwards and wagged his head.

* * * * * * * * * *

Then there was the fellow who was so worried about his job. He said, "I'm fed up, it's all work, day in and day out, week in and week out, year in and year out. It's work, work, work." I said, "When do you start." He said, "Tomorrow."

He would have committed suicide, only it was to permanent.

* * * * * * * * * *

A man crossed a Crocodile with a Budgie. As he was putting the result in it's cage, it bit his leg off and said, "Who's a cheeky boy, then?"

* * * * * * * * * *

NEWS   A Chemist's Shop was broken into last night, and every thing was stolen except hair cream and birth pills. The police are looking for a Bald Headed Catholic.

* * * * * * * * * *

A man said to his doctor, "I've come about these tablets you gave me to keep my strength up . . . I can't get on the top of the bottle."

I saw Murphy at the airport throwing bread to the helicopters.

The other day he found six empty milk bottles in a field. he said, "Look, a cows nest."

* * * * * * * * * *

Trying to find a place to live is terrible. I saw an advert in the paper the other day – "Man in iron lung willing to move over."

* * * * * * * * * *

Thieves escaped from Cork, with over £600,000 from a robbery. Police are still trying to find a motive for the crime.

* * * * * * * * * *

Marriage is a mutual partnership. The husband's the mute one.

* * * * * * * * * *

Most women make appointments for the plastic surgeon. My wife was committed.

* * * * * * * * * *

There's a new Birth Control Pill for Catholic women. It weighs 2 tons. She pushes it against the Bedroom door and her husband can't get in.

* * * * * * * * * *

Murphy has never seen his wife naked. She always undresses in the dark. The Cat is the only one at his house, who knows what she looks like.

* * * * * * * * * *

By the bright silvery light of the moon
PARODY

The world now to-day is getting small they say,
We can travel all around it all too soon,
So now they are going to chase away up through outer space,
To the bright side of the moon.

Do the little men in Mars drive around in Motor Cars?
Have their flying saucers got a Cup and Spoon?
But men, I'm pleased to say, way above the Milky Way,

That they have no Women Drivers on the Moon.

I think they should think twice before they send up little mice,
To see if there is life up in that Gloom.
Cause if the Moon is made of Cheese, Well, Now I ask you Please,
They will surely now start nibbling off the Moon.

Now a recent photograph of the Moon all made us laugh,
The Russians, they are claiming it too soon,
Once upon a time in a favourite Nursery Rhyme,
That little cow jumped right across the Moon.

Instead of Bangor or Portrush next year, you will find a crush,
They say it will be booked right from June,
So ring the Tourist Board before the prices will have soared,
For an all in holiday up on the Moon.

On earth, we seem spellbound, with this Stereophone sound,
Long playing records, now are all the tune,
But Crosby or Pat Boone they say, can't even Croon,
With the voice of the man up in the Moon.

Congrats Barry McGuigan, our local Championship Boy,
But that won't be the end, he will also defend,
His title against the Champion of the Moon.

* * * * * * * * * *

Things are going from bad to worse so quickly now – that the Good Old Days were only last week.

* * * * * * * * * *

A man died last week after falling into a vat of Guinness – it took the Undertaker three days to wipe the smile off his face.

* * * * * * * * * *

I was looking for a girl who didn't smoke, didn't drink and didn't keep asking for money or clothes. I found one yesterday – she was nine.

* * * * * * * * * *

I was going to give up smoking, but coughing's the only exercise I get.

* * * * * * * * * *

I've got so many bills, my place looks like a duck farm.

My wife said, "Why don't you go out to work" but, that's the coward's way out.

* * * * * * * * * *

The Jone's live in a district so posh, even the police station is ex-directory.

* * * * * * * * * *

Picasso was burgled some years ago. They said to him, "Can you describe the man? "Describe him? I'm the great Pablo Picasso." He went away and came back with a drawing of the man. Within two hours, police had arrested two toilets, the Eiffel Tower and a one-eyed chorus girl.

* * * * * * * * * *

Did you hear about the poor Russian family?
They were so poor, the mother had to take in brain-washing.

* * * * * * * * * *

I used to go out with a school mistress. It didn't work out though. If I arrived five minutes late for a date, I had to go home and get a note from my mother.

* * * * * * * * * *

Last Christmas I gave the wife the present she'd always wanted . . . twin beds . . . mine's in Connemara, and, her's is in Cork.

* * * * * * * * * *

Finnegan went into a Wine Shop and asked for a bottle two feet long and one inch wide . . . he wanted to make some rhubarb wine.

* * * * * * * * * *

Murphy fell from the top of the ladder into a cement mixer, they couldn't find the body, so out of respect, they buried three blocks of cement.

I'm not joking. If poverty was a blessing in disguise, his disguise was perfect.

* * * * * * * * * *

I've got a new cure for colds . . . prune juice. It may not cure your cold, but, you certainly think twice before sneezing.

* * * * * * * * * *

Finnegan's not a hard drinker . . . he finds it easy.

* * * * * * * * * *

He's been out of work so long, the last insurance stamps put on his card had St. Patrick's head on them.

* * * * * * * * * *

His main trouble is that his wife dominates him. It's been so long since he opened his mouth, the only language he knows is Latin.

* * * * * * * * * *

He's tried for many jobs. He even auditioned for the film "The Invisible Man", but nobody could see him in the part.

* * * * * * * * * *

You can tell Christmas is almost upon us . . . there are Easter Eggs in the shops.

* * * * * * * * * *

I bought her a new type of space-age cooker. It's all automatic. A button to press to turn it on – and when the meat's done it turns off. There's a button for the toast, a button for stews and a button for vegetables. The trouble is that she's such a bad cook, last night I came home and she'd burnt the buttons.

* * * * * * * * * *

She's got her own way of roasting turkeys. She puts two in the oven at the same time. A big one and a little one.
When the little one starts to get burnt, she knows that the big one is ready.

* * * * * * * * * *

Casey was feeling desperately ill, so he went to the doctor. He said, "I've got one foot in the grave." The doctor said, "Hop it".

* * * * * * * * * *

My dog took a bite out of the milkman.
"Did you put anything on it?"
"No, he ate it as it was."

* * * * * * * * * *

Feeling pretty desperate recently, I tried to drown my troubles in drink. It didn't work. I couldn't get my wife into the barrel of Guinness.

* * * * * * * * * *

A window cleaner working on the 984th floor of the Empire State Building, slipped and plummeted 2,000 feet into his bucket of soapy water.

His friend, Patrick Fitzpatrick, quickly assessed the danger, and said, "Go in after him someone – he can't swim."

* * * * * * * * * *

Miss Murphy, a spinster, came home to her flat one night and found two men hiding under her bed.
She said, "I'll give one of you ten seconds to get out".

* * * * * * * * * *

The Government have found a great new way to get rid of the smoke nuisance in Dublin. It's a law that says all chimneys must inhale.

* * * * * * * * * *

A pal of mine met me in the bar. He was rubbing his nose which was bloated and red. I said, "What's the matter with your nose, then?" He said, "It's my seenus." I said, "Your seenus? You mean your sinus?" "No", he said, ordering a stiff brandy, "I was in the house, see, kissing this girl, see, and all of a sudden her husband came in and he seen us."

* * * * * * * * * *

Murphy's wife worried that he didn't get on with her mother. "I wish you two would hit it off together,' she pleaded. He said, "We should be able to after Christmas, we're buying each other a shillelagh."

* * * * * * * * * *

Mulligan walked into the psychiatrists office. "I keep imagining that I'm a bottle of porter," he said. "Take off your hat and sit down," said the psychiatrist. "Take me hat off?" repeated Mulligan in amazement. "Sure, I'll go flat if I do that."

* * * * * * * * * *

The self-important executive came home to find that his dinner wasn't ready for him. "This is ridiculous!" he stormed. "I think I'll go to a restaurant." "Wait for five minutes," said his wife. "Will my meal be ready then?" "No. But I'll be ready to go with you to the restaurant."

* * * * * * * * * *

How can you tell the age of a chicken?" "By the teeth." But a chicken has no teeth!" "No but you have!"

* * * * * * * * * *

His wife had put a chicken in the oven before she went down to the shop, and she had asked her husband to put another shilling in the meter if the gas went out. he forgot about it. The gas had been out for some time when the chicken peeped out of the oven and said, "Look – either put a shilling in the meter or give me back my feathers!"

* * * * * * * * * *

Judge to Murphy: "What made you think that you could park your car there?" Murphy said "Well, there was a big sign that read: 'Fine for Parking'".

* * * * * * * * * *

Little Paddy's mother had brought him to the Zoo. As they moved through the crowds, Paddy got lost, and, his mother ran around frantically searching for him. Eventually, she found him – in the lion's cage. "Come out of there at once" she said. "Don't you know that's a very dangerous place to be?" "It's twice as dangerous out there," said Paddy. "The lion has escaped."

* * * * * * * * * *

Little Paddy had just got a new baby sister and a neighbour asked him what the baby's name was. "We don't know," said Paddy, "She can't talk yet."

* * * * * * * * * *

After the wedding the bride said to her new husband, "Darling, I have a confession to make. I can't cook." "Don't worry. I have a confession to make too. "I have no job – so there won't be anything to cook."

* * * * * * * * * *

Two small boys were having a discussion about heaven: "If I die first" said Pat, "I'll come back and tell you what it's like" "Promise me as well that you'll come back in the daytime."

* * * * * * * * * *

Teacher: What is the one-twentieth part of three-sixteenths?"
Small boy: I don't know Sir, but it's hardly worth worrying about".

* * * * * * * * * *

Paddy's little cousin from the city was visiting them and Paddy was showing her around. "Oh", she said, "there's a cow! But why hasn't it got horns?" "Well," says Paddy, "some cows don't grow any horns and some have them cut off – but the reason that cow has no horns is because it's a horse."

* * * * * * * * * *

Attacked by two muggers, the young man fought back valiantly. Finally, after a furious battle, the robbers subdued their victim. Then went through his pockets and came up with a total of 20 pence. "You mean to tell me" asked one, "That you fought like that for 20 pence?" "Gosh," the fellow said. "is that all you wanted? I'd have given you that. I though you were after the five hundred pounds I've got in my shoe."

* * * * * * * * * *

My father used to say, "Sing a song everybody understands" So here's a number entitled, Don't play marbles with father's glass eye, he wants it to look for work.

* * * * * * * * * *

All my family were in show business. Everywhere they went they made a show of themselves. Mother used to walk the tightrope. She came to a sticky end. One night she was tight and the rope wasn't.

* * * * * * * * * *

Murphy worked in a circus. They dressed him up in an ape skin and put him in a cage. He tried to fly from one swing to another, missed, and landed in the lions cage next door. He looked at the lion and shouted, "Help! Help! The lion shouted – "Shut your gob or you'll get us both the sack" It was Casey.

* * * * * * * * * *

Poor Casey, he'd turn his hand to anything. In fact he was on the dole so long the Labour Exchange used to send him a card every Xmas.

* * * * * * * * * *

Casey's house was so dirty, you had to wipe your feet coming out.

* * * * * * * * * *

Hear about the fellow who always sat in the rear of the aeroplane, because, he never heard of a plane backing into a mountain.

* * * * * * * * * *

I just flew over from Ireland. "My arms are killing me."

* * * * * * * * * *

On the way over, the pilot was explaining that the entire plane was electronic. He said, "This is the latest device, a talking down machine, it is infallible" He said to the machine, "What time is it" the machine answered back "11.30" He said "You ask it a question. So I said, "Where is my father" The machine said, "Your father is at Portmarnock, playing golf." I said, "That's wrong for a start, my father is dead" The pilot said, "This machine has never made a mistake before, rephrase the question" So I said, "Where is my mother's husband?" The machine said, "Your mother's husband is dead, Your father is playing golf at Portmarnock."

* * * * * * * * * *

The other day Murphy was digging a hole, the foreman said, "Jump out, Jump in, Jump out" Murphy said, "What's the idea", "What's the idea", The foreman said "Your bringing out more dirt on your boots than you are with the shovel."

* * * * * * * * * *

I saw a fellow with his two feet bandaged. I said, "What happened". He said, "I bought a tin of soup and read the instructions" It read, "Puncture lid and stand in a pot of boiling water for half an hour."

* * * * * * * * * *

My mother opened a letter from her daughter in London, and said "My God, our daughter has become a prostitute" My father said, "Thank God, I thought for a minute you said a Protestant."

* * * * * * * * * *

The other day Murphy bought six bottles of whiskey, to celebrate his wedding, and lost them. He dashed into the police station and said, "Did a fellow carry in six bottles of whiskey?" The sergeant said, "No, but the fellow who found them has just been carried out."

* * * * * * * * * *

The last time I was in London, it was a very foggy night. I was making my way home when I bumped into a young lady. I said, "I'm sorry madam," and she said "I'm sorry sire. Well I knew by her accent, she was Irish, so we got chatting. With that, a policeman walked by and shone his torch on us and said to me, "Your under arrest", the next day at Court, the Judge said to me, "Did you kiss this lady`in public" "If I did," says I, "the young lady was my wife." The Judge, "There's no law against that, Case dismissed. As I was leaving the Court the copper said, "sorry I didn't know it was your wife," I said "I didn't know myself, until you shone your torch on us."

* * * * * * * * * *

Which reminds me my dog is sick, and there's nobody at home to bite the postman.

* * * * * * * * * *

When Murphy went on a holiday he was like Columbus. He didn't know where he was going. And, when he got there he didn't know where he was. And, when he returned, he didn't know where he'd been. As he walked past a block of flats, a woman fell from the eight storey into a dustbin. Murphy said, "fancy throwing that out, at home she'd be good for another ten years."

Hear about the Irish vampire? Used to fly into people's houses at night and give blood.

* * * * * * * * * *

Murphy was sitting at home the other night, and the phone rang. He picked it up and said "How should I know, I wasn't in the Navy" he just hung it up. It rung again, he said, "I've just got through telling you, how should I know," just then his wife called out from the kitchen, she said "Darling who's that", Murphy said, "I don't know, some fool keeps ringing up to know is the coast clear."

* * * * * * * * * *

Murphy was digging a big hole the other day, he was about twelve feet down, when an old lady shouted down to him, "It must be very pleasant working and listening to the bells chime from the church", "What's that", said Murphy, she said "Working and listening to the bells chime", Murphy said, "Sure I can't hear a word your saying, with these flipping bells."

* * * * * * * * * *

Heard about the fellow who's cat was as sick as a dog.

* * * * * * * * * *

Casey met his friend, and said, "Aren't you working today?" He said, "No, I'm off sick". Murphy said, "I'm sorry to hear it. What's the matter with you?" He said, "Nothing, but you know how short-sighted our doctor is. I got some spaghetti and stuck it on me legs and told him I had varicose veins. He gave me a fortnight off." Murphy said, "That's a good idea, I'll try that myself." So he went off to the supermarket and bought a tin of spaghetti hoops. He stuck them on his legs, and went off to the doctor. It didn't work. The doctor called the police. He thought it was a shotgun wound.

* * * * * * * * * *

"Waiter! Waiter! That steak was too rare, it just gored my wife. I'm not complaining, I'm re-ordering!"

* * * * * * * * * *

I've got a split personality. Half of me thinks I'm a failure and the other half knows it.

* * * * * * * * * *

There's an Irish micro-chip now. You feed it information you don't need and it forgets it for you.

* * * * * * * * * *

Hear about the Irish man who bought a new pen, because, the old one couldn't spell.

* * * * * * * * * *

Hear about the Irish jeweller who chrome-plated gold bars to make them look expensive.

* * * * * * * * * *

This woman was so houseproud, she was always polishing and sweeping and cleaning. One day she heard noises in the walls. So she called the council in. They had a look round and told her; "You've got rats. The place is over-run with them!"
She said, "Rats! that's impossible! I'm always sweeping and cleaning – I never let a crumb fall on the floor." They said,

"That's where you have gone wrong. The rats think it's a health farm – they come here to loose weight!"

* * * * * * * * * *

An Irish spy. They told him his phone was bugged, so he poured disinfectant down it.

* * * * * * * * * *

Hear about the two crocodiles who robbed a bank and fled the country disguised as handbags.

* * * * * * * * * *

The wife went to a beauty parlour. They called the police immediately. It took her an hour to persuade them she didn't have a stocking over her head.

* * * * * * * * * *

It is a little know fact, that jogging was invented by a drunk. Only in those days they called it staggering.

* * * * * * * * * *

Doctor said to a fellow "I have some bad news for you, you've only got 6 months. to live." Fellow said, "That's alright, when I hurt my back you only gave me a fortnight."

* * * * * * * * * *

It's amazing how many people make their own wine and beer these days. And, they will insist you have a bottle.
Trouble is, just after you drink it, they phone you up, and say, "You haven't drunk it yet, have you?" So you go pale and start to tremble and you say, "Why do you ask?" They say "Oh, no reason, only the enamel just fell off our bath."

* * * * * * * * * *

Murphy's fighting days were over. He committed matrimony. "I've a wonderful wife" he said. "I wish to goodness, I had three or four more like her."

He proposed in a garage, and he couldn't back out.

Murphy reckoned that a wife, was a combined domestic servant, incubator and hot water bottle.

He used to say passion was a feeling you feel when you are going to feel a feeling you have never felt before, and, that kissing was sabotage before invasion.

He said marriage kept you poor, and he should know. Last winter he had to have rubber pockets put in his trousers, so he could steal soup for the kids.

At one time he had a big farm in Ireland. The farm was so big that, when you gazed out across the meadows, all you could see was miles and miles of nothing but miles and miles of miles.

Murphy was married twice. The second time he married his wife's sister. He said it saved him the trouble of breaking in a new mother-in-law. The first time the crows and rooks saw her they got such a fright, they brought back the corn they had stolen three days before.

* * * * * * * * * *

You cannot do a kindness too soon, because you never know how soon it will be too late.

* * * * * * * * * *

There is only one thing wrong with the younger generation; a lot of us don't belong to it any more.

* * * * * * * * * *

Tact is the unsaid part of what you think.

* * * * * * * * * *

No matter how great a man is, the size of his funeral usually depends on the weather.

* * * * * * * * * *

My pal Murphy, he keeps me laughing. The other day he was telling me a story in a railway carriage. A gentleman jumped up and said, "How dare you tell that story before my wife". "I'm sorry, Sir" said Murphy, "I didn't know your wife was going to tell it."

* * * * * * * * * *

Heard the story of the Irishman on trial for his life. He was so eloquent that at the end of his speech, the Judge got 20 years.

* * * * * * * * * *

Before I went abroad, the wife and I decided to have a photo taken. The photographer said he'd like a natural pose, so the wife posed with her hand in my pocket, but it wasn't natural enough, the wife had her mouth closed.

* * * * * * * * * *

The best way to make your dreams come true is to wake up.

* * * * * * * * * *

Nothing is impossible to the fellow who doesn't have to do it himself.

* * * * * * * * * *

The feeling of having done a job well is rewarding; the feeling of having done it perfectly is fatal.

* * * * * * * * * *

I went to the doctor because I was not feeling too well. He said "I have very bad news for you, you only have three minutes to live" I said, "My God! three minutes, what can I do in three minutes". He said, "Sure you could boil an egg."

* * * * * * * * * *

This other fellow went to the doctor, and was told he had only eight hours to live. So the fellow called up his friend and said "I am around here in the doctor's room, and he has given me eight hours to live." His friend said, "Hold on and I will be around to see you." When his friend arrived, they decided to go out on the town. They had drink, girls, more drink and more girls. They were wandering down the street at about 2 o'clock in the morning and his friend said "I have got to get home, I have had enough of this." The other fellow said, "Oh, please do not leave me now." The friend said, "Well, it's all right for you, you don't have to get up in the morning."

* * * * * * * * * *

Father once said to me:
So you want to be independent son., You want to spread your wings,
You want to go to unknown lands, to see what travel brings.
You want to sail across the sea, to smell the ocean tang.
To see those ancient hallowed lands where once the tocsin rang.
Or see the mighty pyramids, on Egypt's golden sand.
Or in the shadow of ancient Rome perchance you want to stand,
Or is it China calling, son, the east with all its glamour?

Or India with its teeming folk, its harsh
discordant clamour?
Or do you want to travel west across the
broad Atlantic,
To wander through the U.S.A., then to
the South, romantic,
To sail the mighty Amazon, through
regions unexplored,
Or through the warm Caribbean seeking
pirate's hoard.
I know son just how you feel, I too, once
felt the same,
The thrill of seeing unknown lands
meant more to me than fame.
I've sailed around the vicious Horn
where a boat can't help but toss,
And I've seen the famous Barrier Reef
under the Southern Cross.
Ah! Yes, I've seen the world. I, too, was
once a rover,
But the greatest thrill I ever knew was to
see the cliffs of Dover.
To know that once again I'd see the glory
of my Sire Land,
The rolling fields, the stately oak, and the
lanes of dear old Ireland.
And so, my son, I've seen the world, no
more I want to roam,
one thing these lands can never be, and
that my son is Home.

* * * * * * * * * *

A miserable looking man questioned by St. Peter on his arrival at the Golden Gate. "Tell me," said St. Peter "about your life on earth?"

Man: "I was a good fellow, St. Peter, really I was. I never smoked, drank or gambled. As regards women, I never went near one during the whole of my life."

St. Peter: "I think you had better go next door, you could do with some excitement."

* * * * * * * * * *

"Some people are funny," mused the man at the bar. "I know a man who hadn't kissed his wife for ten years: then he goes and shoots a fellow who did."

* * * * * * * * * *

Paddy was not feeling too well, he had to go to the hospital to have a heart transplant, and, he sent a get well card to the donor.

* * * * * * * * * *

America is a strange country. I was there last year and this fella asked me if I would like to go to a barbecue. A barbecue, sure I did not know what that was. Its a strange country. They eat outside and they go to the toilet inside.

* * * * * * * * * *

He puts vitamins in his whiskey. He does it so that he can build himself up, whilst he is tearing himself down.

* * * * * * * * * *

An Irish man was struggling along in the black-out when the figure of a m a n loomed nearer. Pat stopped him and said "Can you tell me which is the other side of the road?"
"That's it over there," replied the stranger.
"I thought so," remarked Pat, "Some darned fool over there just told me this was it."

* * * * * * * * * *

"Have you seen my shoes anywhere darling?
"No, precious. Are you sure you had them on when you took them off?"

* * * * * * * * * *

Murphy: "Did you hear about the fellow who stayed up all night figuring out where the sun went when it went down?"
Casey: "No, what happened?"
Murphy: "It finally dawned on him."

* * * * * * * * * *

Galway Bay

Parody

Ah! shure maybe some day I'll go back to Ireland,
If it is only when the wife has passed away,
For God knows the way she used to nag me,
For she had a mouth as big as Galway Bay.

See her drinking 16 pints of Arthur Guinness,
And then her walking home without a sway,
If the sea were beer instead of salty water,
Sure she would live and die around by Galway Bay.

See her sitting at the bar in Paddy Murphy's.
And when the barman says it is time to go,
Sure she does not stop to answer him in Gaelic,
But speaks a language that the clergy do not know.

Now her face was like a pork chop cut in pieces,
And her hair was like a rick of last years hay,

Sure her nose was like a light house out in Claddagh.
That would guide the sailors into Galway Bay.

On her back she has tatooed the map of Ireland,
And when she takes her bath on Saturday,
When she rubs the Sunlight soap down by Claddagh,
You can see the suds roll into Galway Bay.

* * * * * * * * * *

Now little Murphy was growing up,
A fine young man was he.
One day his fond mamma said "Murphy,
Just listen lad to me."
"This world is full of evil things,
With hot temptation rife.
I think it's time, therefore ,you knew
Some of the facts of life."
"I don't know how I can explain,"
She blushed – shame made her pause.
Then in a rush the words came out,
"There is no Santa Clause."

* * * * * * * * * *

Some women were having a chat and, naturally, they talked about their husbands and how helpful they were about the house. One woman said, "My husband is a great do-it-yourself man.

When I ask him to fix something he says "Do it yourself."

* * * * * * * * * *

"My first husband had much more sense than you have."
"I don't see it dear, We both married you."

* * * * * * * * * *

Murphy: "Casey old man, I've noticed lately that my wife's lipstick tastes differently from other ladies."

Casey: "Yes I've noticed it myself."

* * * * * * * * * *

Guide (showing a party of tourists round Dublin): "This is the other side of the building you are looking at, the front is round at the back."

* * * * * * * * * *

The husband was a terrible man for the drink, and his wife had a most unhappy life. In desperation, she went to the priest for advice.
"No matter what I say or do," she complained, "It makes no difference. I give out to him every night he comes home drunk. I send him off to bed

without any supper. But he still goes out the next night and gets sloshed all over again."

"Maybe, you are using the wrong tactics," said the priest. "I think you should try being nice to him. Let him see how good a wife you are and maybe he'll have more consideration. Now when he comes home tonight, have the house nice and warm and a good hot supper ready for him. Meet him at the door with a kiss and let him see that you really care for him."

That night the husband came home in his usual condition. She met him at the door with a kiss, brought him into the warm house, got his slippers and set a lovely steak supper before him.

"'Tis grand, " said he, as he tucked into his steak. "I only hope nobody ever tells my wife about it!"

* * * * * * * * * *

A timid little man went to the doctor and asked for some sleeping pills for his wife.
"But I gave you sleeping pills for her last week," said the doctor.
"I know," said the little man, "but she's after waking up again."

* * * * * * * * * *

A London street musician played "Danny Boy": on his violin and an old lady went up to him and said,
"Hearing that tune made me cry."
"Are you Irish?" asked the fiddler.
"No," she said. "I'm a musician."

* * * * * * * * * *

Casey's car had been destroyed by fire and he went to his insurance company to collect.
"We won't give you the money," he was told, "We'll replace the car."
"If that's the way you operate," said Casey," please cancel that insurance policy on my wife!"

* * * * * * * * * *

"Bingo has given me some of the happiest evenings of my life."
"I thought you never went to bingo?"
"I don't – but my wife does."

* * * * * * * * * *

Four women friends were discussing a neighbour who had just been convicted of dangerous driving. But one of them, Mrs Kelly, said charitably, "None of us is perfect. I have a little failing too. I gamble on the horses." "And I," said Mrs. Cassidy, "am a secret drinker." "I have a very embarassing failure," said Mrs. O'Hara, "I am a kleptomaniac. Every time I go into a supermarket I steal something." "My failing," said Mrs Jackson, "its gossiping. The minute I hear anything juicy, I have to tell everybody. Goodbye, dears".

* * * * * * * * * *

"I hear Mrs. Murphy next door is leaving.: "Good riddance! She's a contrary creature. Where is she going?"
To stay with one of her sons-in-law."
"Which one?"
"I don't know. They both want her to go. The one in Cork wants her to go to the one in Limerick–and the one in Limerick wants her to go to the one in Cork."

* * * * * * * * * *

Mrs. Malone's new neighbour, a very refined lady, called to say hello. While Mrs Malone made some coffee, little Mary, aged six, kept the visitor in chat.
"I like your furniture," said the caller.
"Oh yes," said Mary. "It's lovely. I think the man we bought it from is sorry he sold it. he's always calling and wanting it back."

* * * * * * * * * *

A customer in a rather tatty cafe said to the waitress, "Is this tea or coffee you've brought me?" "Can't you tell from the taste?" "No", "Then what difference does it make?"

* * * * * * * * * *

"Did you see today's newspaper?" O'Shea asked a workmate. "No. What was in it?" "My lunch."

* * * * * * * * * *

"What was the dinner like last night?" "If the soup had been as warm as the wine, and the wine as old as the chicken, and the chicken as fat as the hostess, it mightn't have been so bad."

* * * * * * * * * *

The newly-married husband came home and found his wife putting the finishing touches to a pie in a huge baking dish. "That will last us for a month," he remarked. "What is it?" "It's rhubarb pie." she said. "I know its very big, but I couldn't get any shorter stalks."

* * * * * * * * * *

As the mayonnaise said to the refrigerator – "Close the door, I'm dressing."

* * * * * * * * * *

I just got a bill from my dentist, and, across it was written "THIS IS JUST ONE YEAR OLD"
I sent it back with another notation – "Happy Birthday."

* * * * * * * * * *

We had a terrible row on the wedding day, about the wedding pictures, she wanted to be in them.

I'm so excited. I just won a weekend in Miami with a beautiful blonde! Can you imagine that? A week-end in Miami!

* * * * * * * * * *

But, that is the way it goes – Women have curves and men have angles.

* * * * * * * * * *

Medical science has definitely proven that you cannot milk a cow with a monkey wrench.

* * * * * * * * * *

Every day I have lunch in the pawn shop.
I have to, my teeth are in hock.

* * * * * * * * * *

I was working in my garden when a little
boy called. He had a barrow load of
manure. "Want this manure, Mister,
only £1". "O.K. son", and I gave him £1.
Away he went, next day he was back again
with another barrow load of manure.
"hey, Mister, Do you want this one too?"
"O.K. son". He emptied it into the
garden. "That will be £4" he said "Oh, Oh,
son, the first barrow load of manure was
only £1, why £4 for this load?" "Well you
see Mister, somebody stole my shovel last
night, so this load is all hand picked."

* * * * * * * * * *

Old woman in the street shaking Bed
Blankets – a shocking thing to do,
especially in a tough local district. I
shouted to her, "Hey Ma, you wont kill
them all that way." "Maybe not son, but
I'll sure make them dizzy for tonight".

* * * * * * * * * *

I am very keen on dog racing. I bought a racing dog. But what a lazy brute he was. Would not run, and, could hardly walk. So I decided to take him to the Veterinary Surgeon, he gave me two large pills, a red pill and a green pill. He said, "Take the dog home, give it the green pill first, then the red pill." Well to make a short story longer, I took the dog home and it had no sooner swallowed the green pill, when it was out the door and away up O'Connell Street, like a rocket. Do you know – if I had not taken the red pill myself, I would never have caught him.

* * * * * * * * * *

Of course my friend never had a haircut in his life, he was not an eccentric, just bald. I said to him, "Why do men go bald?" He said, "It's caused by the activity of the brain, the same reason why women do not grow beards."

* * * * * * * * * *

Nature gave her a beautiful face, but she picked her nose herself.

* * * * * * * * * *

I hear the Russians are just crazy about licking postage stamps. It's the only way they can stick their tongues out at the Government.

* * * * * * * * * *

Of course I could tell you a terrific story about an engagement ring. But, it is too near the knuckle.

* * * * * * * * * *

You know there are important things we should ask ourselves. Did you ever think – do the people in Glaucomara wonder how things are here?

* * * * * * * * * *

Somebody sent my mother over 2 big boxes of tea bags from America last Summer. She stayed up one night cutting them open. When she was finished she had 347 piles of dust on the mantle piece. They got mixed up with my Uncle Jack's ashes, and somebody made tea with them. My mother said "Oh! that is your uncle Jack allright, he always made a lovely cup of tea."

* * * * * * * * * *

Four U.N.O. soldiers were standing at a street corner. An Englishman, an Irishman, an Arab and of course an American. A beautiful girl passed by. The Arab said, "By Allah", the Englishman said, "By Jove", the Irishman said "Be Japers", and the American said, "By Saturday."

* * * * * * * * * *

I call Jersey City girls, "Toothpaste", because, I can squeeze them in the tubes."

* * * * * * * * * *

I saw Murphy the other day, with his arm in a sling. I said, "Why the arm, I thought you broke your leg." He said, I thought I'd look silly with my leg in a sling."

* * * * * * * * * *

An Englishman, An Arab and an Irishman, having a drink at the same bar. The Englishman said: "Speaking of families, if I had one more boy in my family, I would have enough to have my own football team, already having 10". The Irishman said "I have 14 boys in my family, one more and I would have my own rugby team". The Arab said, "I have

17 and one more and I would have a golf club."

* * * * * * * * * *

Any guy who would take advantage of a girl is a RAT – Would somebody please pass me the cheese.

* * * * * * * * * *

This perfume is so seductive – they give away a police whistle with every bottle.

* * * * * * * * * *

Then I saw the hand writing on the wall – I was in the Men's Room at the time.

* * * * * * * * * *

Murphy was always unlucky with the girls. No matter who he brought home, there was always something wrong with her. If she was blonde, his mother would say "Oh they are dizzy". If she was a black head, "Oh they are dull". And a red head "Oh they are fiery" Murphy went out one night and saw a girl who was the image of his mother, brought her home and his father hated her.

* * * * * * * * * *

Here in Ireland we are going to send a man to the Sun. I said "You will be burnt alive" he said "Don't worry we are going up at night."

* * * * * * * * * *

I have had a terrible two weeks. I nearly lost my wife – what a Poker game that was.

* * * * * * * * * *

My wife has just had major plastic surgery – I took her credit cards off her.

* * * * * * * * * *

Now they are printing newspapers on cellophane. It's just great for restaurants. You can read and watch your coat at the same time.

* * * * * * * * * *

I know a guy who laid down on the track of the (local) railroad to commit suicide. It was very sad – he died of old age waiting for the train.

* * * * * * * * * *

All the guards at the asylum carry monkey wrenches. That's in case a nut gets loose.

* * * * * * * * * *

Marriage is a funny thing – with some marriages the only thing left that people have in common, is that they got married on the same day.

* * * * * * * * * *

A mixed marriage in Ireland, is when a Protestant marries a Catholic. When you are having the reception, you have to invite the Vicar and the Priest. I asked the priest "Would you like a drink". He said he would and had a whiskey, I then asked the Vicar, who said, "I would rather commit adultery than have a drink." "Oh," said the priest, "I did not know I had a choice."

* * * * * * * * * *

A couple were married for 60 years. On the day of their wedding anniversary, the wife decided to go to town to the beauty salon to have her hair and face done, AND AFTER 60 YEARS YOU KNOW IT WOULD NEED SOME DOING. While she was in town, her husband found a box in the bedroom. In it were two eggs and a thousand pounds. When his wife returned home he asked her about it, and she said: "Every time I was unfaithful to you, I put an egg in the box." The husband thought – "well it's not too bad, after all we are married for 60 years and there are only 2 eggs in the box." He said, "That's O.K., but, where did you get the money?" She said, "Every time I got a dozen eggs, I sold them."

* * * * * * * * * *

An American priest visited to Ireland – He was staying with an old lady in a wee cottage and he noticed that there was no clock on the mantlepiece and no calendar on the wall. So he asked her how she told the time of day. "By the sun, Sir", she said. "Fair enough, but how do you know what day it is" he asked. She said, "That's simple. There's the day we go to church, and the day after. Then there's the day we go to the fair and the day after. The day before the day we don't eat meat, the day we don't eat meat and the day after."

* * * * * * * * * *

But come here till I tell you. Where I come from . . . Dublin . . . The weather is wonderful. The air is so invigorating in our village, the caretaker of the cemetery walks around all day with a shilellagh, saying, "Lie down, boys, lie down there."

* * * * * * * * * *

All the years I've been in Ireland, I've never kissed the Blarney Stone. Last week I went to Blarney especially, walked up 200 stone steps, only to find it was the caretaker's half day. But an old lady sitting there explained to me, that all the girls in the village had kissed the stone, so if I kissed one of the girls it would be the same as kissing the stone. Well, come here till I tell ye . . . walking down the road, I met a little smasher. She was wonderful. Do you see what I'm coming at? I told her exactly what the old lady had told me. I asked her for a kiss. "Sir", says she, "To tell you the truth, I never kissed the Blarney stone, but I often sat on it."

* * * * * * * * * *

Murphy's room in London, was so damp, he caught a fish in the mouse trap.

That was because of the wash hand basin, there was no bottom to it. But it was very handy, as you could wash you hands and feet at the same time.

Next door was the bridal suite. It was the only room in the house with a lock on the door. During the night he heard a voice say: "Darling you hair is beautiful, it should be guilded. Your lips are beautiful, they should be guilded. Your arms are beautiful they should be guilded." He couldn't stick it any longer, he knocked on the door and a voice said "Who's there", Murphy said, "A Guilder from Dublin."

* * * * * * * * * *

Murphy sayings:

Never get drunk in the first Bar . . . always wait until the last and its not so far to get home . . .

She speaks through her nose – her tongue is worn out . . .

No more weddings for me – my fighting days are over . . .

That's the whole kettle of fish in a nutshell . . .

* * * * * * * * * *

It was Casey's job that caused it, he worked as a lion tamer in a circus. He worked under the name of Claude Bottom.

His mother-in-law was in the act too. The lion used to put his head in her mouth.

I saw him the other day, he was looking years drunker. His wife was the trouble, he caught her posing nude for a painter. He was doing a Murial.

Now he's starting to smoke in bed. His wife complained, she said, "You never used to smoke in bed before we were married."

But their's was an intricate love affair. I'd like to explain that to you. A rather big girl named Short, fell in love with a short little man named Long, whilst Little little thinking of short, fell in love with a short little lass named Long. Well, in order to make a short story long, Little proposed to Long, thus, making Short long to get even with Little's short comings.

Well it so happened that Short meeting Long threatened to marry before Long, well this made Little marry Long before long.

But the question is, did big Short love Little less because Little loved Long. Well, that's the long and the short of it like a couple named Long who got a divorce; they couldn't get along together.

* * * * * * * * * *

One liners:

ROMANCE: Is like Insurance. Costs more as you get older.

ALIMONY: It's just an old wives tale.

BANKRUPT: He could not tell the difference between stocks and blondes . . .

BEAUTY PARLOUR: Where the talk alone is enough to curl your hair.

TROUBLE: I'm in desperate trouble with a married woman . . . My wife . . .

DIVORCE COURT: Where the cream of society go to be separated.

* * * * * * * * * *

Did I ever tell you about the time Murphy was farming, and he broke his plough. His wife said, "Go and ask Casey for the loan of his." he said, "What's the use, he'll only refuse." She said, "You don't know until you've tried, and we need a plough, so go and ask him." Off he went to Caseys farm, five miles distant, he kept saying. "He wont lend it, and he'll tell all the boys in the village how I trudged five miles in the pouring rain, and, he refused, and they'll all laugh their heads off." By this time the rain was coming down in bucket fulls, he was drenched to the skin, and up to his knees in mud. He kept saying to himself: "I know he wont lend it." He said, "Look what happened to Dooley, Casey made a laughing stock of him. Just because, Dooley asked him for the loan of a field to plant spuds in. He's had a chip on his shoulder ever since." With that he arrived at Casey's farm, walked up through the haggard, soaked to the skin. he knocked at the door, Casey threw the half door open – THE BOTTOM HALF – Casey shouted, "What do you want." Murphy said, "I want to tell you" says he, "What you can do with your plough."

* * * * * * * * * *

Murphy was so lazy ... even as a baby his mother used to have to suck his thumb. Always in trouble, he told me he sold his bicycle for twelve pounds. I said, "That was a good price." He said, "Yes, but the fellow didn't pay me, and what's more, had I known he wasn't going to pay me I'd have charged him twice as much."

* * * * * * * * * *

Heard about the fellow who crossed a chicken with a banjo, so it could play itself.

* * * * * * * * * *

Heard about the fellow who objected to his daughter leaving a convent, to marry a former priest. He said, "It was bad enough to have a sister as a daughter, without having a father as a son."

* * * * * * * * * *

My wife said marriage was almost like being in love. I said, "When I have a shave in the morning, I feel 20 years younger." She said, "Why don't you have a shave before going to bed at night."

She eventually left me. It broke me up. I might say it took me at least two days to get over it.

Murphy's wife left him. It really broke him up. He was inconsolable. he said, "I really loved her." I said, "Well, don't worry another women will turn up and you'll fall in love with her." He said, "I know that, but what am I going to do tonight."

* * * * * * * * * *

The Lord said to Moses, "Wilt thou take the Commandments," Moses said, "How much are they." The Lord said, "They're for free." Moses said, "I'll take ten."

* * * * * * * * * *

A policeman walked up to a suspect with two suitcases and said, "What's in that case." The suspect said "Sugar for my tea." "And what's in the other case." The suspect replied "Sugar for my Coffee." So, the copper gave him two taps on the head with his batton. He said, "What's that for?" The policeman said, "That's two lumps for your cocoa."

* * * * * * * * * *

A man's not old when his hair turns grey, and a man's not old when his teeth decay. But, a man is old, and will sometimes weep,
when his mind makes an appointment that his body's can't keep.

* * * * * * * * * *

A caterpillar becomes a silkworm, a silkworm becomes silk, silk becomes a dress, a dress becomes a girl, a girl becomes a wife, a wife becomes a mother, a mother becomes a mother-in-law, and a mother-in-law becomes a damn nuisance.

* * * * * * * * * *

My wife's mother was so small, she had to stand on a box to wipe her nose.

* * * * * * * * * *

She made her own yoghurt, she put a glass of milk on the table and just stared at it.

* * * * * * * * * *

I said, "Can I have your daughter for my wife," she said, "What does your wife want with my daughter."

Some women are naturally ugly, but she abused the privilege.

* * * * * * * * * *

A great big fellow walked into a green grocers and said to the assistant, "I'd like half a cabbage," the assistant said, "We don't sell half a cabbage." The big fellow started to argue, so the assistant walked over to the boss, not knowing that the big fellow was behind him, and said, "I'm having a bit of trouble with a dirty, big mouthed, six foot eejit, who wants half a cabbage," when he turned and saw your man standing behind him, "And this gentleman would like the other half."

* * * * * * * * * *

I saw a sheeps heart in a butcher's shop – I walked in and said "How much." The butcher said "1.57" I said, "I only want it for dinner, not a transplant."

* * * * * * * * * *

Murphy's hobby was growing vegetable marrows, and Murphy had the biggest marrow in the village and every night before going to bed, he covered it up carefully, so the frost wouldn't get at it. So, this particular night he woke up, looked out the window, put on his pyjamas, and, went out to cover it from the frost, and that was how they found him in the morning. FROZEN TO THE MARROW.

* * * * * * * * * *

Dr. Paisley arrived at the gates of heaven and was stopped by St. Peter, who said, "You can't come in unless you've done something outstanding on earth." Mr. Paisley said "I'm the only Orangeman who ever walked down the Falls Road waving a Union Jack, and singing, God Save the Queen on St. Patrick's Day." Peter said, "And when did this happen," Paisley said "About two minutes ago."

* * * * * * * * * *

My wife brought me home to meet her mother. She was so ugly, if Moses had ever seen her, he'd have made another commandment.

Moses wasn't so clever – had he turned left in the desert instead of right, the Jews would have all the oil, and, the Arabs all the oranges.

* * * * * * * * * *

I must say, I came from a very unusual family. Father suffered from music on the brain, when he was young, somebody hit him over the head with a saxophone.

Mother played the piano on board the Titanic – THAT WENT DOWN WELL

We were very poor. So poor we got food parcels from Bangladesh.

Mother couldn't afford to buy us boots for school, she used to paint out feet black and lace up our toes.

One day she sent me with my twin brother to the butchers for a sheeps head and said: Tell him to leave the legs on, and leave the eyes in, it will see us over the week-end." I said, "Would you have a few bones for the dog." My brother said,

"Goody, goody, are we going to get a dog."
The butcher felt sorry for us, took his
apron off and said, "Take this home and
make a stew out of it."

* * * * * * * * * *

Murphy got a job digging a garden that
hadn't been cultivated for years, there
were stones, thistles, nettles six feet high,
but Murphy got dug into it and six
months later, you wouldn't have
recognised it. He'd everything growing
there. Potatoes, Spuds, Cabbage, Bacon,
the lot. Well one evening, the old Parish
Priest was passing, stopped, and looked at
the garden and said: "Mr. Murphy, it's
wonderful – with a wee bit of help, what
God can do for a garden." "It is indeed",
said Murphy, "But, you should have seen
it when he had it to himself."

* * * * * * * * * *

Three little boys playing. One said "My
Daddy is the bravest man in Dublin.
Yesterday he dived into the canal and
saved three little boys from drowning."
The second boy said "That's nothing, my
Daddy saved an old man and woman
from being burned to death in a top flat in
Ballymun." The third boy said "My
Daddy is a terrible coward, when Mammy

went to hospital, he was so nervous he had to get the woman next door to come in and sleep with him."

* * * * * * * * * *

Casey came out of hospital unexpectedly. His little boy was home, the mother was out shopping. He said, "How has everything been going since I was away?" The kid said, "Mr Murphy has been in every might, and last night he brought a bottle of whiskey." Casey said, "Say no more! When your mother comes, I'll ask you the same question, and you tell me all over again, Right." That evening, when his wife came in, he worked round to the question and said, "Did anybody call while I was in hospital?" The kid said "Yes, Dad, Mr. Murphy was here most nights, and last night he came in with a big bottle of whiskey, Dad, and after they drank it all, he started to kiss and cuddle my Mammy, just like you used to do with my auntie Lizzie, when Mammy was in hospital."

* * * * * * * * * *

Three Ministers of the Church out shooting. A Parish Priest, A Rabbi and a Protestant Bishop. Passing a lake, a pheasant rose. The P.P. promptly shot it down, knelt for a couple of seconds and said some prayers, looked up into the sky, blessed himself, then ran straight across the lake and retrieved the bird. A few minutes later another pheasant rose, the Rabbi shot it, knelt down, said a few prayers in thanksgiving, then dashed across the lake. About ten minutes later a third bird rose, SOME BIRDS NEVER HAVE ENOUGH the Protestant Bishop raised his gun, fired and down went the pheasant. The old Rabbi nudged the P.P. and said, "Don't tell him where the stepping stones are."

* * * * * * * * * *

Did you ever see such weather in all your life. The rain was pouring down. Do you realise that an hour of this weather at this time of year, will do as much good in five minutes, as a month of it would do in a week at any other time of the year.

* * * * * * * * * *

As one fellow said to the other "If we all get into this bus, it will not hold the half of us.

And always remember, that the greatest disaster in the world can be followed by an even greater one.

* * * * * * * * * *

Fellow went to the doctor and said, "Can you help me out?" The doctor, said, 'Yes, which way did you come in."

He said, "I'm a kleptomaniac." The doctor said "Have you tried taking anything for it."

The doctor said, "Put your tongue out. . . Don't put that back in your mouth, you'll poison yourself.

The doctor said, "Put your right foot up on the table, put your left foot up as well" and Murphy fell flat on his back . . . "Your getting those dizzy spells again" the doctor said.

Murphy said, "It's the brother, he's sick. The doctor said: Remember, he only thinks he's sick". Off Murphy went and returned four days later. The doctor said, How's your brother", Murphy said, "he thinks he's dead. The doctor said "Is he sure", Murphy said, "I hope so, we buried him this morning."

* * * * * * * * * *

A fellow walked into a Newsagent and asked for the evening paper. The Newsagent said, "This will cost two pence extra tomorrow" The fellow said "Then give me half a dozen."

A fellow was ironing his pants when the phone rang: He put his hand up and burned half his ear off.

* * * * * * * * * *

He was told to fix the leak in the thatch, unfortunately, when it rained, it was too wet to get up and fix it. But when it stopped raining he couldn't find it.

He bought a horse, but couldn't get it to hold its head up. The fellow who sold it said "it's only pride, he'll probably hold his head up when you pay me for him."

* * * * * * * * * *

Pat walked into a green grocer, and said, "Half a stone of potatoes, and give me the small ones – the big ones are too heavy to carry."

Son to father – "Dad, have I got a big head?" "No, son, of course not, now just run down to the village and get me a stone of potatoes." "What will I put them in?" "Put them in your cap, and take my bike." "I can't ride it Dad, it's too high." "Then let some air out of the tyres."

Guard walked up to three fellows standing at the corner and said "If you three want to stand there – ye had better move on."

* * * * * * * * * *

Pat travelling home by train, got out and looked pretty sick. I said "Felling unwell" He said, "I always get sick when I sit with my back to the engine." I said "Why didn't you change places with the fellow sitting opposite you." He said, "I couldn't, there was nobody sitting opposite."

* * * * * * * * * *

When Pat came to Scotland first, as he was getting off the boat, there was a diver coming up a ladder at the quay side. "Well," said Pat, "That beats all, here I am after paying my fare and there's a fellow after walking it."

* * * * * * * * * *

Pat thought he'd like a job as a diver, so he went to the harbour and applied. he was told he would have to see the foreman, who was on the ocean bed, so Pat threw off his coat and dived in – he came up the first time and gulped, and when he came up the second him he shouted to Mike, "If I don't come up a third time you'll know I've started." He got the job, but he did not like it. He couldn't spit on his hands.

* * * * * * * * * *

Pat was complaining to his wife, that Murphy's hens and roosters were keeping him awake all night. So he dashed into Murphy's house, came back and said to the wife. "Well, everything's fixed, I've just bought all the hens and roosters off Murphy and put them in our yard – Now, let Murphy stay awake all night."

* * * * * * * * * *

A fellow walking home from a fair with a duck under each arm, came to the cross roads, and there was a young girl crying her eyes out. She said "I'm afraid to go up that lane in case I'm assaulted." he said, "I'll take you up," she said, "You might assault me," He said, "How, with two ducks under me arm." She said, "Couldn't I hold the DUCKS."

* * * * * * * * * *

Casey went to a Fair, as he had promised to show his 14 children the prize Bull. Tickets were 10p each, he said "I can't afford it." The fellow said "Are all these kids yours? Casey said, "Yes." The fellow said "Well hold on, and, I'll bring the bull out to have a look at you."

* * * * * * * * * *

Pat and Mike got drunk one night. Pat said to Mike, "Come down to the harbour, I'm going to Canada." So down they went, Pat got into a row boat and said to Mike, "Throw off the rope Mike." Mike did so, but the rope caught on a hook. Pat started to row and Mike fell asleep. Well, about four hours later he woke up, and there was Pat still rowing away. He shouted, "Pat! Hello! Pat!" Pat looked up, shook his head and said, "Who the blazes knows me in Canada."

* * * * * * * * * *

The doctor gave Casey some pills and told him "take two after a hot bath." The next day the doctor said, "Did you take the pills," Casey said, "No – I haven't finished the hot bath yet."

The doctor said, "Take these pills, and take two every second day for a week. You understand – you take two on Monday, skip a day, two the next and so on." he went back the weekend and the doctor said, "Did the pills do you any good?" Casey said "Yes, but the skipping damn near killed me."

The doctor said, "You want a good rest – so I suggest you sleep in one room and the wife in the other. Fix a bell over your wife's bed, and should you feel lonely, just press the button and the bell will ring in your wife's room. And tell me about it tomorrow" He was back again the next day. The doctor said "Did it work?" He said, "No – every hour during the night the wife kept coming in waking me up and saying "Did you ring."

* * * * * * * * * *

My wife is so fat, that when she gets into bed, I roll towards her. I have to sleep on the inside. The other night she gave me a quick dig in the ribs with her elbow, she said "You've changed. When we were first married and in bed, you were so romantic, so frivolous. Don't you remember. You used to bite the tips of my fingers, my ears, my neck." I said, "For Gods sake woman, your speaking of forty years ago", she said, "Please do it again," I said, "O.K. Pass me my teeth."

* * * * * * * * * *

THE RAGGED JACKET

If life were a thing that money could buy,
The rich would live and the poor would die,
But, God in his Goodness, has made it so,
That the rich and poor to the grave must go.
So when I'm dead and in my grave,
With one hundred years to back it,
Who then will know which were the bones,
That wore the Ragged Jacket?

So, here's success to the working man,
May his tyrants wear a frown,
May his beef and his beer increase each year,

May his wages never go down.
May his dear little wife be the pride of his
life,
And, never kick up a racket,
But, do all she can, to please her old man,
And, patch up his old Ragged Jacket.

* * * * * * * * * *